How to Win at
POKER

ACKNOWLEDGEMENTS

Thanks to:

Joe Holtaway, my inspiration for this story.

Jill Ryan and Yvonne Hobson for their generous insights.

Dave Muir from Sennen Surfing Centre and Mesha Wardman, lifeguard and surf live-saving champion, for their guidance and encouragement.

Patch Harvey, Coxswain of the Penlee Lifeboat, for his time, patience and expertise.

And to Polly Lyall Grant, my editor, and Twig, and everyone else who's spurred me on to write this book.

Needless to say, any mistakes are unquestionably mine!

This book is dedicated to the work of the RNLI, the true heroes.

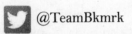 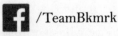
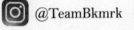 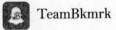

How to Win at
POKER

Belinda Levez

TEACH YOURSELF BOOKS

For UK order queries: please contact Bookpoint Ltd, 39 Milton Park, Abingdon, Oxon OX14 4TD. Telephone: (44) 01235 400414, Fax: (44) 01235 400454. Lines are open from 9.00 – 6.00, Monday to Saturday, with a 24 hour message answering service. Email address: orders@bookpoint.co.uk

For U.S.A. & Canada order queries: please contact NTC/Contemporary Publishing, 4255 West Touhy Avenue, Lincolnwood, Illinois 60646 – 1975, U.S.A.. Telephone: (847) 679 5500, Fax: (847) 679 2494.

Long-renowned as the authoritative source for self-guided learning – with more than 30 million copies sold worldwide – the *Teach Yourself* series includes over 200 titles in the fields of languages, crafts, hobbies, sports, and other leisure activities.

British Library Cataloguing in Publication Data
A catalogue record for this title is available from The British Library

Library of Congress Catalog Card Number: 96-72624

First published in UK 1997 by Hodder Headline Plc, 338 Euston Road, London NW1 3BH.

First published in US 1997 by NTC/Contemporary Publishing, 4255 West Touhy Avenue, Lincolnwood (Chicago), Illinois 60646 – 1975 U.S.A.

Typeset by Transet Limited, Coventry, England.
Printed in Great Britain for Hodder & Stoughton Educational, a division of Hodder Headline Plc, 338 Euston Road, London NW1 3BH by Cox & Wyman Ltd, Reading, Berkshire.

Impression number   13 12 11 10 9 7 6 5 4
Year   2002 2001 2000 1999 1998

CONTENTS

INTRODUCTION

Poker is a game which is easy to learn and fun to play. Most people learn to play poker at home with family and friends. The stakes are often low, just piles of matchsticks and your pride. However, playing for money, especially with strangers, is an entirely different experience.

You may have found yourself in the following situation: You are at a party/gathering and get chatting to a stranger. "Can you play poker?" he asks. The question seems innocent enough, and he appears friendly, so you answer "Yes" and find yourself invited to play a game. You are introduced to the stranger's friends who warmly welcome you. You feel relaxed and confident, especially after you've won the first couple of pots, but then your luck changes. A few hours later your wallet is lighter and you are wiser. You have learnt that playing poker is easy but winning money at poker is not. You also no longer trust your new friends. You begin to wonder whether or not they were cheating. Some of the hands you were dealt were really good but your opponents always managed to have even better hands. You have just had your first real poker lesson and it cost you a lot of money.

To play poker well takes skill, knowledge and lots of practice. This book aims to teach you how to win at poker. You will be shown the basic principles of the game, and given advice on where to gamble and the associated costs involved. The dangers of playing in private games with strangers are also highlighted and you are shown how to spot cheats. You will be taught how to get better value for money and methods of play that maximise winnings whilst keeping losses to a minimum. Popular variations of the games are described and strategies given for each game which you should adapt according to the strengths and weaknesses of your opponents.

Lots of illustrated examples are given to make the understanding of the games easier. A glossary is included to define the jargon used in the book and some of the additional jargon that you may encounter.

By the end of this book you should be a more informed player with a better understanding of the game. With plenty of practice you should also become a more skilful player and, hopefully, a winner instead of a loser. Good luck!

1

WHAT IS POKER?

Poker is a name given to a huge number of card games. What they have in common is that they are based on the ranking of five card hands. The basic game is relatively easy to learn. The object of the game is to win the money bet by having the best ranking hand. Poker is mostly played with cards, but versions using dice also exist. The games can be played with a minimum of two players but around five to seven players is more practical.

The rules of individual games vary enormously. The number of cards dealt to each player, the methods of betting and the ranking of the hands can all differ. Even games of the same name will often be played in a variety of ways. It is therefore important to ensure that you fully understand the rules before you start playing.

In private games you play against all the other players. In order to win you need to beat all of your opponents. Each player takes turns at being the dealer.

When you play in a casino, you have two options. You can either bet against other players or against the casino. In the former, the casino supplies the dealer, charging a percentage of the pot (the money bet) for this service. A deduction of around ten per cent is common. Alternatively, the casino may make an hourly charge for the use of their facilities. If you decide to play against the casino, the casino is the banker and pays out all bets at fixed odds.

Why play poker?

The main attraction of poker is that it is a game of skill. With many card games you rely totally on the luck of the deal. If you have a good hand you win, if you have a poor hand you lose.

Poker is entirely different. Even if you have the worst possible hand you can still win the game by skilful bluffing – you fool the other players into thinking that you have a good hand.

Poker relies on a good player being able to outwit his opponents. You will need to assess the other players' strategies and make decisions based on your conclusions whilst trying to conceal your own strategy. You will constantly appraise your opponents, looking for signs that tell you whether or not they are bluffing, whilst ensuring that you do not let them guess your likely hand.

A good player can increase his winnings by using strategies which keep other players betting for as long as possible. You will need to decide if your opponents are luring you into betting or whether they are just being cautious. Other strategies rely on forcing players to fold by raising bets. Here you will need to consider why a particular player is raising the stakes. Is it just a scare tactic or does he really hold a good hand? You need to consider how much information you are giving away when you bet. Your decisions will usually be based on experience about what you have learnt about the way your opponents play. All the time you will be assessing your own hand, calculating your chances of winning and deciding your next move.

Taking a sensible approach to gambling

Before you begin gambling, you should work out a financial budget. Calculate all your household and living costs including savings. Realistically work out how much money you can comfortably afford to lose – yes *lose*. Gambling is risky, not everyone wins, and there are plenty of losers. You can easily lose all of your capital. Be aware that there are much easier, more profitable and safer ways of making money.

Once you have decided your budget, make sure you never go over this limit. If your personal circumstances change, be sure to re-calculate. If you spend only disposable income on gambling, you won't encounter many problems. However, if you start betting with your rent money and lose it, you may be tempted to try to recoup your losses by betting more heavily. This is the route to financial ruin.

When you play, take only your stake money and enough for your expenses (fare home, drinks, meals etc). Leave all cheque books and cash cards at home. If you can't get hold of more money, you can't spend it. Don't be tempted to borrow money from friends, and be sure to decline all offers of credit. If you run out of money, either go home or just spectate.

If you don't want to carry large amounts of cash, open a separate account for your gambling money and take with you only the cheque book and cards relating to that account when you gamble.

Exchanging money for chips

In most games, particularly in casinos, you exchange your money for chips. You don't play with 'real money', just a pile of plastic discs. Psychologically the value of your money diminishes. When you see a bank note, you associate it with its true value – you appreciate how long it would take you to earn that amount of money and what you can buy with it. As soon as you exchange it for chips, those associations disappear. It is no accident that chips resemble coins – coins are considered almost worthless. It's easy to pick up a pile of chips and put them on a bet. If you had to count out bank notes, you would certainly be more cautious.

When you decide to play, don't immediately change all of your money into chips. Instead, change it in small amounts. If you have to keep going to your wallet, you will have a better appreciation of how much you are losing as you will be watching real money diminish rather than chips.

If you win, it's all too easy to give your winnings back by continuing to play. If you are playing in a casino, as soon as is convenient, go to the cash point and change your cash chips back into money. Once you see the true value, you will be more reluctant to carry on betting.

People like to have piles of chips in front of them – it makes them look like a high roller. Walk around a casino and see the proud smiles when someone has a big pile of chips. However, you should only have in front of you the amount of chips that you need to play.

——— What does it cost to play? ———

Once you have calculated your budget you need to find a game that is compatible with your level of stakes. If the stakes are too high you will find yourself quickly running out of money.

The minimum amount of capital you need varies depending on the game. As a rough guide, the capital needed for a game of draw poker is around forty times the minimum stake. With seven card stud approximately fifty times the minimum stake should be sufficient. Games like hold 'em and omaha need around one hundred times the minimum stake. By dividing the amount that you have budgeted for by the minimum capital required, you can find the minimum stakes that you can play for.

The minimum stakes on many poker games are low. You should be able to find somewhere to play to suit your budget. You don't have to be a high roller to go to a casino. Most casinos have plenty of low stake tables. If you prefer to play in private games, you should be able to find one that suits your level of stakes.

Do not aim too high when you are still learning. Even if your budget allows you to play in the more expensive games, stick initially to the cheaper games and gradually work your way up. Remember, the higher the stakes the better the players.

Additional costs

It's all too easy to go over your budget by forgetting to include all the costs. Casino gambling has additional hidden costs which include things like:

● house advantage
● commission
● admission charges
● membership fees

- travelling costs
- refreshments
- your time.

Commission

Casinos charge gamblers for the use of their facilities. With poker, a percentage of the pot is taken by the house. This is a small price to pay when you consider that you are guaranteed a fairly run game. Around ten per cent is the usual deduction. For bigger games players are often charged an hourly rate for their seat.

House advantage

In games where the casino acts as a banker, a hidden charge is made for the privilege of betting. Many people don't even realise that there is a charge for gambling. On many games like Caribbean stud poker you are not paid the true odds. The casino reduces the odds paid to allow it to make a profit.

—————— Finding your game ——————

It is a good idea to try playing a variety of games at home. Decide which game you like the best, and once you have selected your favourite concentrate solely on that game. Try to watch as many games as possible – you can learn a great deal by watching experienced players. If someone is winning, try to determine why. Are they just lucky or are they using a particular strategy? Are their stakes varied or constant? What do they do when they lose – do they increase or reduce their stakes or stop playing?

Check the rules before you start playing

Learn how to play a game before you bet on it. This may seem common sense, but a lot of people start playing poker with no understanding of the rules. Often they are introduced to poker by friends or relations and they simply bet in the same manner as their friends. They end up learning by their mistakes which can be costly.

Remember, the rules of poker vary enormously. Ensure you fully understand all the rules before you play. Casinos will have written copies of their rules available. Take them home and study them at your leisure. If you don't understand them, ask for an explanation. Whatever game you select, find out as much information about it as possible.

You need to be particularly careful with private games as rules may differ enormously. Just knowing the name of a game is not sufficient as players often introduce variations.

Have a full discussion about the rules before you start playing. It is often a good idea to write down the rules that you have been told to avoid later disputes about what was actually said before play commenced.

Pay particular attention to the ranking of hands as you may find that hands other than the standard rankings are permitted. Ensure that you fully understand the method of betting and whether or not checking is allowed (see page 14). Agree both minimum and maximum bets. If wild cards are used, check if additional hands like five of a kind count in the ranking.

The lollapalooza

John Lillard's poker stories (1896) recounts the tale of a cheat playing a game of poker in a Montana saloon. He deals himself a hand of four aces and ends up betting against an old prospector. The prospector bets all of his money against the cheat. When the hands are revealed the prospector only has an assortment of clubs and diamonds which is not a ranking poker hand. The cheat starts counting his winnings, only to be stopped by the old man. He explains that a lollapalooza beats any other poker hand and that three clubs and two diamonds is in fact a lollapalooza. The other players agree with him so the cheat concedes the win. Later in the game, the cheat deals himself a lollapalooza. He bets heavily on his hand. At the showdown he reveals his hand expecting to take the pot. He is then informed that he should ask the rules before playing as a lollapalooza can only be played once a night.

Get plenty of practice

You need to be able to immediately recognise the value of your hand and where it comes in the ranking. Deal out hands of five cards, identify the poker hands and put them in the correct ranking order. You will soon appreciate how infrequently a good hand is dealt. Once you have mastered the ranking you can then start to judge whether or not a hand is worth playing.

Get plenty of practice. Take a pack of cards and deal out dummy hands as if you're playing the game with several players. Look at your own hand. Decide whether or not it is worth playing. Then assess your hand against the others. Did you make a good decision? Would any of the other hands have beaten yours? Are you throwing away hands that could easily win? By continuing to do this you will learn the sort of hands that are worthwhile playing and those that are not.

Play alone or with friends until you are familiar with all situations. Practise placing bets as you play. Some games are played so quickly that it can be difficult for a novice to follow them. With practice you will become faster.

As mentioned earlier, it is important to play at the right level. Don't aim too high when you are still learning. Stick to the cheaper games and gradually work your way up. Remember, the higher the stakes the better the players.

2
PLAYING TIPS

Poker relies on the other players not knowing your hand. Although the other players cannot see your hand, the way that you react to its contents can give them a lot of information.

Body language

Suppose you have a really good hand. It is quite likely that as you look at the cards you will smile, raise your eyebrows or constantly look at your cards. You know that this time you are certain of a winning hand. When you're excited your voice also changes. The other players will notice and probably fold, meaning that your good hand will win you very little money.

If, alternatively, you have a poor hand, you are more likely to frown. You may decide to try bluffing, but if you appear nervous, fidgety or start playing with your chips, the other players are less likely to believe you. You may even give one of the classic signs of lying, such as touching your nose. When you are nervous you are also more likely to stutter.

People who have complete control over their mannerisms make better poker players. If you can look at your cards and show no facial expressions whatsoever you make it impossible for other players to glean any information about your hand. When you look at your hand, memorise its contents. Pay attention to your mannerisms – don't fiddle with your chips or your jewellery. Stay calm, even if you have a royal flush. If you play and bet confidently you are more likely to intimidate the other players.

One of the most difficult reactions to control is blushing, but you can use this to your advantage. Ask other players direct questions about their hands. If you correctly guess their hand they may blush. However, be prepared for other players to ask you questions. A confident reply may confuse them.

Keep records

Keep records of your gambling. A small note book is sufficient to keep records of how much you win and lose. Most people tend to remember the big wins and forget the losses. After each game write down the reasons why you won or lost. Analyse the results and learn from your mistakes.

If you lost, try to determine why. Were you staying in when you should have folded? Were you folding with hands that could have won? Were you failing to force other players into folding? Was your body language giving away information?

When you win also try to determine the reasons why. Was it because your strategy was good? Were you just dealt lots of good hands? Did other players make stupid mistakes? Were you picking up on any signs given by the other players?

Periodically analyse your records. They will tell you if you're sticking to your budget and if your betting strategy is effective. Proper records will make you aware of any weaknesses. You can then alter your strategy to compensate.

Player profiles

If you play regularly with the same people, try to build up a profile of each one.

- What sort of hands do they bet heavily on?
- What forces them to fold?
- How often do they bluff?
- Does their body language give any clues?
- How do they bet with a good hand?

Try to work out each player's strategy.

Appreciate your chances of winning

Many people expect to win but don't realistically assess their chances of winning. With all bets there is the chance that you will lose, and it is important to understand how to calculate your chances of winning. You may decide that a bet is simply not worthwhile.

Learn how to calculate the odds for the game that you are playing. Fully appreciate your chances of improving hands. Before you place a bet, make sure you understand your chances of winning. If you are playing in a casino do not forget to take into account the rake (the charge made by the casino for the use of its facilities).

With banking games find both the true odds (your chances of winning) and the odds paid by the casino. Is there a huge difference? You may decide that it is not worth your while having a bet.

Vary your play

Players use different styles of play. Some play aggressively, continually raising in an attempt to force everyone to fold. Other players are very cautious, throwing away anything that is not a good hand. You will know when they suddenly make a huge bet that they have a good hand.

Try not to stick to one style of playing. The most successful poker players are those who are totally unpredictable. If in some hands you play cautiously and in others aggressively you will confuse the opposition. You should aim to vary your betting, the number of cards you take (if playing a draw game), how often you bluff and the signals that you give.

Know when to stop gambling

It can take an enormous amount of discipline to stop betting, particularly if you are on a winning streak. It is possible to get carried away by the excitement of the game. You may have intended to spend only an hour gambling but you're on a winning streak, so you continue. Because you are betting with your winnings rather than the initial stake money, you decide to place larger bets. Your next bet loses, what do you do? For a lot of people the tendency is to bet more heavily to recoup that loss. This will usually continue until you run out of funds.

If you have lost your stake money, decline all offers of credit. Even if the other players agree to accept an IOU, you should withdraw from the game. Stories abound of people who have run out of money and who have ended up throwing their car keys or the promise of some other asset into the pot. If the stakes are getting too high or you are losing too much, stop playing. By having a sensible approach to gambling you can ensure that you do not lose more than you can afford.

The majority of gamblers are able to keep to their budgets. However, gambling can be addictive for some people so beware. If you start losing more than you can afford, seek help. Details of organisations that can help are given at the end of the book.

Try to decide in advance at what stage you are going to stop betting. Set yourself an amount to win or lose or impose a time limit. Stop playing when you have reached your limit. As soon as a winning streak stops either bet small stakes or go home. This approach will minimise your losses. Other players may complain if you suddenly stop playing, but remember you are not betting for their benefit. Do not feel obliged to give them the opportunity to win their money back.

You should always stop playing if you are tired. You need to ensure that you are concentrating on the game. When you are tired, you take longer to make decisions and are more likely to make mistakes.

It is also wise to avoid alcohol. It tends to slow down your reactions and your ability to think. It also lowers your inhibitions, and makes you less likely to care about losses. You should certainly never play if you are drunk.

3

THE BASIC GAME

One deck of 52 cards with the jokers removed is used. Before any cards are dealt, players make an initial bet called an ante-bet. This helps to increase the pot. It also makes the game more competitive as players are more likely to try to win the pot if they have contributed to it. All the bets are placed in the centre of the table. In casinos, players exchange their stake money for chips. With private games bets are often made with cash but some schools may use chips to facilitate betting.

Each player receives five cards dealt face down. A round of blind betting may take place (players make a bet without looking at their cards). This further increases the pot. Players look at their cards. A round of betting commences starting with the player to the left of the dealer (in forms of poker where some cards are placed face up, the player with the highest or lowest card may bet first).

Each player has the option of betting or folding (withdrawing from the game). A player holding a poor hand may decide to fold. If you fold, your cards are returned to the dealer without being revealed to the other players. You lose any bets made.

Some games allow players to 'check'. This usually happens on the first round of betting after the cards have been dealt. Players do not have to participate in the first round of betting, instead they announce 'check'. If they wish to continue in the game they must bet on their next turn. If all the players decide to check, new hands are dealt to everyone. Some players use checking as a strategy for bluffing. They have a good hand but do not want to make it obvious on the first round of betting. When it is their turn to make a bet, they raise the stakes. This strategy is called 'sandbagging'. However, if you have a fairly decent hand, it can be a risky strategy to check. If all the other players check you will lose out on a pot that you may have won.

The first bet determines how much each player has to bet in order to stay in the game. Players may also raise the bet up to the agreed maximum. Betting continues until either only one player remains or there is a showdown and players reveal their hands. If only one player remains (all the others have folded), he will win the pot. He does not reveal his cards to the other players. If there is a showdown, the player with the highest ranking poker hand wins the pot. In the event of a tie the pot is shared. In a showdown (figure 3.1), player D would win as he has the highest ranking hand.

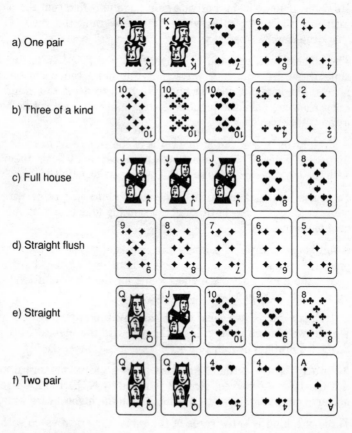

a) One pair

b) Three of a kind

c) Full house

d) Straight flush

e) Straight

f) Two pair

Figure 3.1 Example hands

— The standard ranking of hands —

The aim of poker is to win the pot by having the highest ranking hand. A poker hand is made up from five cards. The more difficult a hand is to achieve, the higher its position in the ranking. Figure 3.2 shows how the hands are ranked.

Each type of hand is also ranked according to the values of the cards. The highest value cards are aces and the lowest are twos. The cards are ranked in the following descending order: A,K,Q,J,10,9,8,7,6,5,4,3,2. The suits do not affect the ranking, so if two players both have a royal flush, one with hearts and one with spades, the hands will tie. However, if you play in a private game, you may find that the players introduce their own rules which differently rank the suits. Always check the rankings before you play.

The highest ranking hand is a royal flush – A,K,Q,J,10 in the same suit. There are only four ways that this hand can be made, with hearts, diamonds, spades or clubs. If you are dealt this hand, you know that you have the highest ranking hand and can not be beaten by any other player.

A straight flush is a run of five cards of the same suit in consecutive numerical order. If two players both have a straight flush, the player with the highest card wins so K,Q,J,10,9 beats Q,J,10,9,8.

Four of a kind is four cards of the same numerical value with any other card. Four aces is the highest ranking four of a kind and will beat four kings.

A full house is three of a kind (three cards of the same value) and a pair (two cards of the same value). Where two players have a full house, the hand with the highest value for the three of a kind wins. So 10,10,10,2,2 would beat 8,8,8,A,A.

A flush is a run of five cards of the same suit in any numerical order. Where two players have a flush, the one with the highest card wins. So J,8,6,5,3 would beat 9,8,6,5,4.

A straight is five cards of any suit in consecutive numerical order. A,K,Q,J,10 is the highest straight followed by K,Q,J,10,9. Where two players both have a straight, the hand with the highest card wins.

Three of a kind is three cards of the same numerical value with two cards of different values. Three sixes would beat three fours.

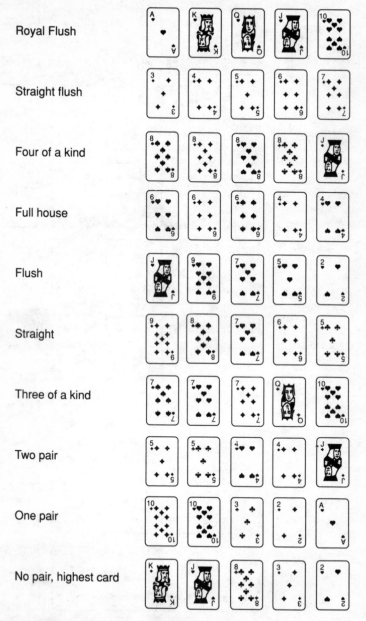

Figure 3.2 Poker hands ranked from highest to lowest

The 'Wheel'
or 'Bicycle'

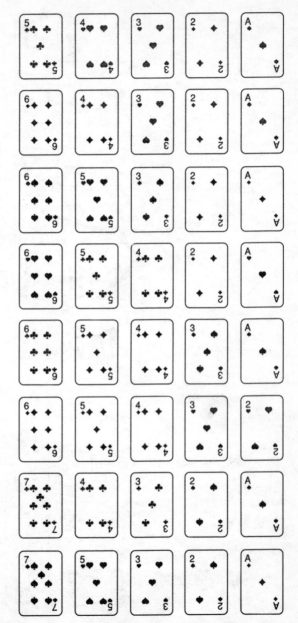

Figure 3.3 The ranking of hands in low poker

Two pair is two sets of pairs (two cards with the same value) with any other card. Where two players both have two pair, the value of the highest pair decides the winner. A,A,3,3,2 would beat 10,10,8,8,A. If both players have the same two pair, the value of the fifth card decides the winner. K,K,Q,Q,8 would beat K,K,Q,Q,4. If all cards have the same value there is a tie. *Aces over eights* (two aces and two eights) is known as the dead man's hand. It takes its name from the last hand held by the infamous gambler Wild Bill Hickock. In the late 1800s, he was playing poker in a saloon at Deadwood, Dakota. He was sitting with his back to the door when he was shot dead by Jack McCall. His last hand consisted of a pair of aces and a pair of eights.

One pair is two cards of the same value with three other cards of different values. A pair of queens would beat a pair of jacks. If two players have the same pair, the hand with the highest value other cards wins. A,A,10,7,5 would beat A,A,9,7,5. If all of the cards are of the same value then there is a tie.

Where none of the above hands is held, the winner is the player with the highest card. In a showdown a hand containing an ace would beat one with a king and so on.

Low poker

The ranking described so far is for high poker. It is also possible to play low poker, where the lowest ranking hand wins – known as the 'wheel' or the 'bicycle'. Other games exist where players compete for both the highest hand and the lowest hand. They usually nominate what hand they are playing for. Here the pot will be split, half for the highest hand and half for the lowest hand.

Figure 3.3 shows how the low hands are ranked. Before playing these games, you should check what the lowest rankings are as they may vary.

Additional rankings

It is always important to check the ranking of the hands before you play as some games include additional hands. In private games you may come across one or more of the hands described below. (See Figure 3.4 for examples.)

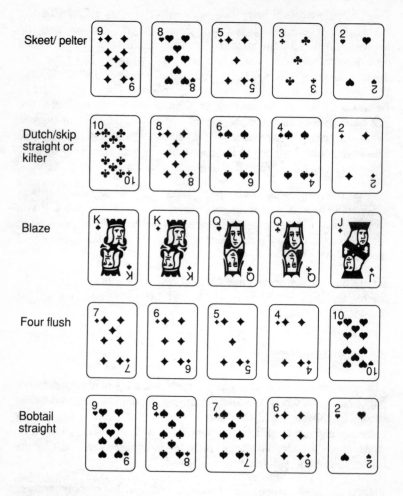

Figure 3.4 Additional rankings

Skeet/pelter

These hands come between a flush and a straight in the ranking. It is commonly 9, 5, 2 and two other cards below 9 of any combination of suits. However, some games specify that the two other cards must include one card between 9 and 5 and the other card between 5 and 2. If the cards are all the same suit, you have a skeet flush which ranks higher than a straight flush.

Dutch/skip straight or kilter

This is an alternately numbered straight. For example, 10,8,6,4,2 or K,J,9,7,5. It ranks lower than a straight but higher than three of a kind.

Blaze

This is a combination of any five court cards that do not contain three of a kind. For example, K,K,Q,Q,J or Q,Q,J,J,K. It ranks higher than two pair but lower than three of a kind. Where this hand is allowed it would, for example, beat A,A,9,9,7.

Four flush

This hand consists of four cards of the same suit, for example, 7,6,5,4 of diamonds and 10 of clubs. It ranks higher than a pair and lower than two pair.

Bobtail straight

This hand consists of four consecutive cards of any suit and ranks below a four flush. For example, 9 of hearts, 8 of spades, 7 of spades, 6 of diamonds and 2 of hearts.

Cats and dogs

The following hands rank between a flush and a straight. If they are permitted, always check exactly where they come in the ranking as their position may vary. None of the hands must contain a pair. (See Figure 3.5 for examples.)

Big cat/tiger

This hand consists of a king and an 8 with three other cards with a value between a king and an 8.

Little cat/tiger

This hand should have an 8 and a 3 with the three other cards having a value between an 8 and a 3.

Big dog

This hand needs an ace and a 9 with the three other cards having a value between an ace and a 9.

Little dog

This hand consists of a 7 and a 2 with the three other cards having a value between 7 and 2.

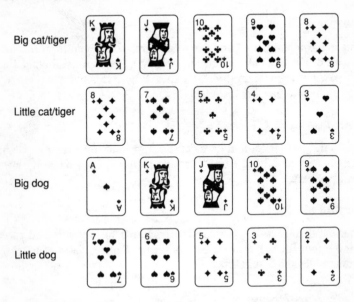

Figure 3.5 Additional rankings – cats and dogs

Five of a kind

In private games, it is common to allow the use of 'wild' cards. A wild card is a nominated card which can be used in the place of any other card. For example, the twos may be declared 'wild'. If you needed an ace to make up a hand, you could use a 2 instead of an ace. Alternatively, one or more jokers may be added to the pack and declared wild. If, for example, you needed a queen to make up a hand, you could use the joker in its place. By allowing cards to be wild, higher ranking hands are easier to achieve.

When wild cards are allowed, an additional hand of five of a kind is also possible (see Figure 3.6). Five of a kind ranks higher than a royal flush. If you are playing with wild cards always check that five of a kind is permitted as some games may specify that the wild card can only be used in place of another card, which excludes this possibility.

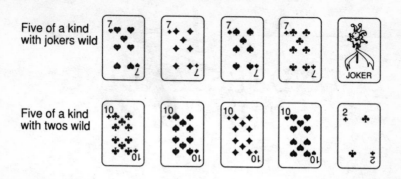

Figure 3.6 Five of a kind

The basic game of poker is easy to learn. This is poker in its simplest form, but it is hardly ever played in this manner. Lots of variations have been introduced to make the games more exciting and challenging. There is a huge number of different games where both the rules and the methods of betting vary. Games of the same name may be played in a huge variety of ways in different locations. Gamblers who play regularly together may also add their own rules to create more excitement.

The number of cards dealt to each player varies with different games. Some games allow the players to improve their hands by taking extra cards, these are the draw games. Other forms exist where some cards are placed face up on the table. Either some of the players' cards are revealed or players use community cards combined with their own cards to make up the best hand. These are the stud games.

4

UNDERSTANDING THE ODDS

In order to play poker well a sound understanding of the odds of being dealt particular hands is essential. With games like draw poker you need to know the chances of improving your hand. As private games incorporate so many variations, it is important to understand how changes in the rules affect the odds.

In standard games of poker 52 cards are used to make five card hands. There are $\frac{52 \times 51 \times 50 \times 49 \times 48}{1 \times 2 \times 3 \times 4 \times 5}$ = 2,598,960 different possible hands.

The likelihood of being dealt a particular hand in poker

Hand	Number of ways hand can be made	Odds against being dealt cards in your first hand
Royal flush	4	649,739/1
Straight flush	36	72,192/1
Four of a kind	624	4,164/1
Full house	3,744	693/1
Flush	5,108	508/1
Straight	10,200	254/1
Three of a kind	54,912	46/1
Two pair	123,552	20/1
One pair	1,098,240	15/1
Highest card	1,302,540	1/1

To appreciate just how rare the higher ranking hands are, consider how long it takes to play 649,740 hands. If you play, for example, an average of one hand every five minutes, you would need to continue playing constantly for approximately six years and two months. By playing for a few hours each week the chances of being dealt a royal flush in your first hand are something short of a miracle.

Take a pack of cards and deal them out into five card poker hands. By continually repeating this you will begin to appreciate just how rare it is to be dealt one of the higher ranking hands. You will start to get some idea about which hands are worth playing. Pairs are very common. Pairs appear very low down in the ranking but a high pair can often be sufficient to win a game.

If poker is played with only five cards dealt and no further cards exchanged for others from the pack, players are mostly competing with low ranking hands. This is one of the main reasons why so many variations exist. By increasing the number of cards dealt to each player or allowing players to exchange some of the cards for new ones from the pack, the chances of having a higher ranking hand are increased. The varied games add more interest and excitement.

_____ How the odds change with _____ different games

Poker can be played in a wide variety of ways. A different number of cards may be dealt and the number of cards players can exchange may vary. To have a good knowledge of the odds for your particular game you need to take these factors into consideration in your calculations. Before agreeing to any change in the rules ensure that you fully appreciate how the change will affect the odds.

Draw games

When you are playing draw poker, you have the opportunity to improve your hand by exchanging your cards for others from the deck. Before betting and exchanging cards, you will want to know your chances of improving your hand so that you can decide if it is worthwhile staying in the game.

You can calculate your chances of improving your hand by comparing the number of ways in which your desired cards can be dealt to the total number of possible ways in which the remaining cards can be dealt.

The chances of improving a hand when three of a kind is held

Suppose your hand is K,K,K,6,3. By exchanging your last two cards, you have the opportunity to make either a full house or four of a kind. For the full house you need a pair and for four of a kind another king is required.

There are four cards of the same value in each suit. Each value can be arranged in six different ways (see Figure 4.1).

Figure 4.1 Ways in which a pair of fours can be made

There are thirteen different values in total, from ace to 2. As you already hold the kings you are left with a possible twelve other values from which to make a pair. A pair can be made in 72 ways ($6\times12=72$). You are discarding two cards which reduces the number of ways a pair can be made by five. You therefore have $72 - 5 = 67$ ways in which you can make a full house.

You currently hold five cards, leaving 47 other possible cards ($52 - 5 = 47$). Even though some of the other cards have been dealt to other players, you do not know what cards they hold, so you need to take all possibilities into account when making your calculations. With 47 cards there are 1081 ways in which two cards can be dealt $\left(\dfrac{47 \times 46}{1 \times 2} = 1081 \right)$.

Your chances of improving your hand to make a full house are therefore $(1081 - 67) / 67$ or $1009/67$ or odds of approximately $15/1$.

To improve the hand to four of a kind you need the last king. By exchanging one card, you are giving yourself odds of $46/1$. By exchanging two cards, your odds of having the king are $46/2$ or $23/1$.

The chances of making four of a kind by drawing three cards to a pair

Suppose your hand is A,A,7,9,4. With three cards there are a possible 16,215 hands $\dfrac{47 \times 46 \times 45}{1 \times 2 \times 3} = 16{,}215$.

The hand you want to be dealt is A,A,X, where 'X' is any other card. A,A,X can be made in 45 ways, where 'X' is any of the other 45 cards.

Your chances of being dealt this hand are $(16215 - 45) / 45$ or $359/1$. You can see that the chances of making this hand are remote.

The chances of making a full house by drawing one card to two pair

If Q,Q,J,J,10 is held, you need either a queen or a jack for a full house. You exchange one card. There are 47 possible cards that could be dealt to you. Four of them would give you the desired hand (the other two jacks or the other two queens) – 43 of them would not. The odds are $43/4 = 10.75/1$.

The chances of making a flush when one card is needed

Suppose your hand is K,9,4,2 of hearts and 10 of diamonds. Your chances of getting another heart to make the flush are as follows: There are nine hearts left which would give you the desired hand and 38 other cards. Your chances of having a heart are $38/9 = 4.33/1$

There is a general rule that says if you get nothing in your first deal you should fold. If you study the table of odds for improving hands you can see the reasoning behind this rule. You may dream of turning a pair into four of a kind but in reality it is very difficult to achieve.

Stud games

In games like seven card stud and hold 'em, a five card poker hand is made from seven cards. With seven cards you are able to make up 21 different five card poker hands. This hugely improves each player's chances of achieving a higher ranking hand. By looking at the cards that each player is showing, or the community cards, you can deduce the possible hand that they may hold and calculate the chances of them having that particular hand.

With omaha, nine cards are used to make a five card poker hand. Therefore 84 different five card poker hands can be made by each player which makes it even easier to achieve a high ranking poker hand.

A pair of aces may have been enough to win a game of five card stud, but in omaha, a pair of aces is highly likely to be beaten.

You are also able to adjust any calculations about players' hands by taking into account the cards that you hold and those which the other players have on display. Consider a game of seven card stud, where four cards of each player's hand are displayed.

A player may have two queens and two jacks displayed. In order to make a full house, he needs either another jack or another queen in his hand. If you have a queen in your hand and another player has a jack displayed, then a full house with queens and jacks can only be made from two other cards, the remaining jack or queen.

If there are five players, 20 cards are displayed, and you also have three cards in your hand. That leaves 29 other cards. Two cards would give a full house. This means the player has odds of 15.3/1 against having a full house $(29 - 2) / 2 = 13.5/1$.

If no jacks or queens were displayed by other players, or in your hand, the odds against him having a full house with jacks and queens would be $(29 - 4)/4 = 6.25/1$. You can see that taking into account the cards held by you or displayed by other players can make a big difference to the odds.

The effect of using wild cards

In some games, wild cards may be permitted. A wild card is a card
that can be used in place of any other card. If, for example, twos were
wild, a two could be used to make up a higher ranking hand (see
Figure 4.2).

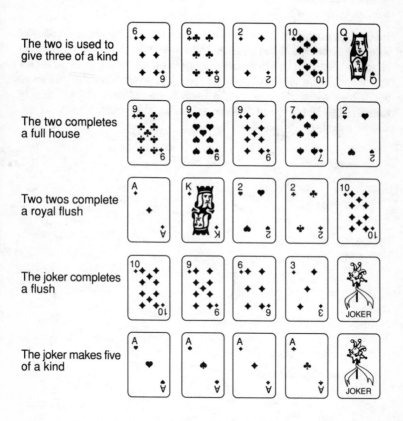

Figure 4.2 Using wild cards

The use of wild cards is common in private games. However, they
drastically change the odds so you need to completely re-think the
way you play the game.

Where wild cards are used, the higher ranking hands are much easier to achieve. Without wild cards, there are only four ways in which a royal flush can be made. By having, for example, twos wild, the number of ways a royal flush can be made hugely increases to 504. The odds of being dealt a royal flush are cut from 649,739/1 to 5156/1. All of the other hands are also more easily achieved. What may have been a good hand in a game without wild cards may be a poor hand if wild cards are used.

Instead of nominating one of the values already in use as wild, the jokers may be added to the pack and made wild. This will completely change the calculations again, as more cards are used. If three jokers are added, the number of possible five card poker hands increases to 3,478,761. The number of ways a royal flush can be made will be 224 compared to 504 if the twos were wild. The odds against a royal flush will be increased to 15529/1.

5

BETTING

—— Developing a betting strategy ——

You need to develop a betting strategy that will maximise your winnings whilst minimising your losses. Your betting strategy also needs to be varied so that the other players can't predict your hand. If you always double the stakes when you have a good hand it will soon be noted by the other players. Players who always bet the minimum possible will immediately advertise their good hand if they suddenly place a huge bet.

From your player profiles you will have a good indication of your opponents' reactions to particular levels of betting. Some players may back down after a modest raise, while others may need a huge raise in order to fold. You will be able to spot the players who are staying in the game simply because it is not costing them very much. Your profile may tell you that one particular player always folds early on when he has nothing. If he is still there in the later rounds of betting, you will know to treat him with caution.

When to raise

The way you bet throughout the game can determine whether you win or lose. See Figure 5.1. Suppose you are playing seven card stud. Your two hole cards (the cards that are dealt face down) are a pair of jacks (Player A). The manner in which you bet early on could be enough to win you the game. If, after the third card is dealt, you make

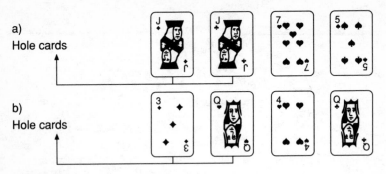

Figure 5.1 Betting strategy – knowing when to raise

a big raise, you may force players to fold who could potentially beat you. After the first three cards, Player B has a poor hand. He would be likely to fold if the stakes were suddenly increased.

However, the situation may be entirely different if you do not raise. Player B may continue playing, simply because it is not costing him very much. He still has the possibility of being dealt another queen. If his fourth card is a queen, he is then in a stronger position. If he then raises after this card, you are in trouble, as you know you do not have enough to beat a pair of queens.

Another situation may arise if you have an exceptionally good hand such as a full house. You want to keep the other players betting for as long as possible to maximise the pot. Large bets early on will just increase the chance of everyone folding. If everyone folds, you only succeed in winning the ante. By placing smaller bets and gradually increasing them you can try to keep more players betting for longer. Your knowledge of the players will determine just how far you can raise the stakes without making them fold.

Bluffing

Just because your hand is poor it doesn't automatically mean you will lose. Having the nerve to bluff and back up the bluff with a heavy round of betting can cause other players to fold, even when their hands are better than yours. Do not expect to win every hand that you play. Bluffing should be used sparingly. If you bluff too often it can work against you. There will be situations where you have a fairly good hand but want to force out a player who you suspect may have a slightly better hand. If you are known as a player who bluffs a lot, your strategy may not work. No matter how much you raise, your opponent will not back down. If, instead, you are known as a player who rarely bluffs, a large raise by you will be taken much more seriously.

Knowing when to fold

Don't stay in the game for too long. If your hand isn't good enough to win, withdraw from the game. By continually staying in for one extra round of betting with a hand that is clearly going to get beaten, you lose more money than you need to. If you are bluffing and the bluff is obviously not working, then fold. It is pointless to keep raising.

Playing in casinos

A sign will indicate the minimum and maximum bets for each table. Before any cards are dealt each player makes a bet called the ante. Players have the option of betting the same amount as the previous player, raising the bet, checking (reserving the right to bet in the next round) or folding. Some games allow players to bet blind. Whatever you decide to do, you must make your intentions clear. To stay in the game you need to bet at least as much as the previous player.

Playing in private games

Private games offer a great deal of flexibility as players can organise the betting in a wide range of ways. It is best to keep to a fairly simple method of betting. If you use a complicated system it can interfere with the game. You have enough to think about without having to perform complex calculations just to determine your next bet.

Whatever system you use, you should always agree a minimum and maximum bet, and the amount of the ante. It is often a good idea to include an ante. This ensures that there is initially some money in the pot which may give the players the incentive to try to win it. Games which do not specify an ante can be slow to develop.

Instead of each player contributing an ante-bet, you may encounter games where the dealer contributes a number of chips to the pot. As each player takes turns in being the dealer, the amount each player contributes evens out over the course of a session.

Using a set limit

With this system, players agree both a minimum and a maximum bet. The range between the minimum and maximum should be fairly wide to give players the opportunity of making decent raises. If, for example, the gap between the minimum and maximum bet is only four chips, it does not give a player much opportunity to force other players to fold. Players will tend to stay in the game simply because it is not costing them very much. If you have a range of around ten chips, a high raise will have more impact. Someone raising the stake by ten chips will be able to force players into folding.

Example of betting using a set limit

Minimum bet – 1 chip; maximum bet – 10 chips; ante – 1 chip
Four players – A, B, C and D

Player	Action taken	Stake	Total in the pot
A, B, C & D	Ante	1 chip from each player	4
A	bets 2 chips	2	6
B	raises 2 chips	4	10
C	bets 4 chips	4	14
D	folds	0	14
A	raises 2 chips	6	20
B	raises 5 chips	11 *	31
C	folds	0	27
A	raises 2 chips	13	40
B	raises 10 chips	23 **	63
A	folds	0	63

Player B wins the pot of 63 chips. His stake was 39 chips.
Net winnings: 63 – 39 = 24 chips.

* Although the maximum bet is 10 chips, this is not the maximum number of chips that a player stakes. Player B's bet consists of a bet of 6 chips to match the previous bet, plus 5 chips which is his own bet.
** Player B matches the previous bet of 13 chips and makes an additional bet of 10 chips

---

Here an ante of one chip has been agreed which means that each player must bet one chip before any cards are dealt. To stay in the game each player must bet an amount equal to the previous player. They can also raise the stakes by betting an additional amount up to the maximum bet.

Straddle method

In this method of betting, the first player makes a bet called the ante. The second player makes a bet of double the ante called the straddle. The cards are dealt. After looking at his cards the third player has two choices. He can either make a bet of double the straddle or withdraw from the game. The other players then take turns to decide whether or not to bet or withdraw from the game. To stay in the game, each player must bet at least the same amount as the previous player. Bets can also be increased, usually up to an agreed maximum. Betting will continue until no one else raises or the maximum bet is reached. The players then reveal their hands.

Example of the straddle method

Ante – 2 chips; maximum bet – 20 chips; opening bet double last straddle

Four players – A, B, C and D

Player	Action	Stake	Total in pot
A	makes ante-bet	2 chips	2
B	doubles ante	4 chips	6
C	opens	8 chips	14
D	calls	8 chips	22
A	folds	0	22
B	raises 5	13 chips	35
C	calls	13 chips	48
D	folds	0	48
B	raises 10	23 chips	71
C	folds	0	71

Player B wins the pot of 71 chips. His stake was 40 chips.

Net winnings: 71 – 40 = 31 chips

Freeze out

With this method of betting, each player has an equal amount of capital at the beginning of the game. The object is for one player to win all the chips. Betting is arranged using any agreed method. When a player runs out of chips, there is an immediate showdown and the player with the highest ranking hand wins the pot.

Running out of money

Occasionally a player may run out of money midway through a game. In this situation a second pot may be opened. The remaining players make all further bets to the second pot. The player with insufficient funds waits until either one player remains or there is a showdown. If one player remains, he wins the second pot. If several players remain, then the one with the highest ranking hand takes the second pot. The hand that won the second pot is then compared to that of the player who has run out of money. The player with the highest ranking hand wins the original pot.

6
CHEATING

Poker is particularly vulnerable to cheating. There are lots of ways in which players can be duped. Playing in legal casinos is the safest way to ensure that the games are fairly played. If you play in private games, you should be aware of the many methods of cheating so that you can ensure that you are not conned.

Betting light

One of the easiest ways to cheat is for players to not fully contribute to the pot. If there are a lot of chips already in the pot, it is not always obvious how many chips a particular player is adding. You may see him pick up the required number of chips, but it is very easy to just drop a few into the pot and palm the rest. Everyone's attention then switches to the next player and the one who palmed the chips is able to discreetly put them back on the table with his own chips.

Alternatively, a cheat may bet so quickly that you do not see what chips he picks up. The only indication that you get of a bet being made is the clinking of chips as more are added.

Marked cards

In poker it is advantageous for gamblers to know what cards the other players are holding. Anyone with this knowledge is able to bet only when he knows he has a winning hand.

The easiest way to accomplish this is to mark the backs of the cards in such a way so that they can be 'read' by the cheat. The designs on the backs of the cards are often intricate patterns. It is possible to add shading, small dots or to slightly thicken lines. These changes will not be noticed by the other players unless the cards are carefully scrutinised.

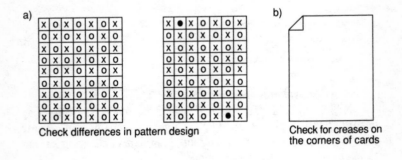

a)

Check differences in pattern design

b)

Check for creases on the corners of cards

Figure 6.1 Cheating using marked cards

Even if someone produces a sealed pack of cards, they may still be marked. It is a relatively simple task to mark the cards and reseal them in their original packing. Professionally marked cards can also be purchased. The designs may be identical but certain cards may have a slightly thicker border on one side.

Before you begin playing you should carefully study the cards. Pay particular attention to the corners. Marks are placed here so that they can be seen when players are holding their cards. Compare the high cards to the low cards. Often only the high cards will be marked.

Cards should also be checked during the course of play as they can become marked either intentionally or accidentally. Most commonly corners of cards can be bent to make creases visible. If any marks are found use a new pack of cards.

Technicians

Dealers can cheat in lots of ways. Someone who is skilled at manipulating the cards is called a technician. It is easy to look at the bottom card whilst shuffling. With practice it is possible to position desired cards at the bottom of the pack. The dealer can then deal his hand from the bottom of the deck and the other players' hands from the top.

Another method is to spot a good card whilst shuffling and to place it on the top of the deck. The dealer saves this card for himself and deals from the second card down to the other players.

A player can also use a spiked ring to make an indentation in the cards. When it is his turn to deal, he simply has to feel the cards to identify the best ones. He can either save them for himself using one of the techniques already described or simply keep track of which player receives them.

Cutting the cards

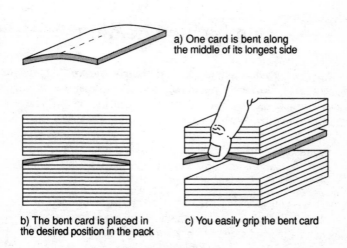

a) One card is bent along the middle of its longest side

b) The bent card is placed in the desired position in the pack

c) You easily grip the bent card

Figure 6.2 How a cheat can ensure that the cards cut in a certain place

To combat cheating by the dealer it is common practice for one of the players to cut the cards. However, the dealer can overcome the problem of the cards being cut by bending one card in the middle so that it is slightly curved. The cards will tend to be cut at the curved card. Try this yourself with a pack of cards – you will find that you easily grip the curved card but the ones below it slip through your fingers. A dealer cannot guarantee that it will work every time but on the occasions when it does, he is guaranteed of a win.

Collusion

With poker, the game relies on players not knowing each other's hands. If two or more people are colluding, they can ensure that their best hand is always played. The player with the poorer hand will simply drop out of the betting.

The colluding players will have a set of signals to tell the other player their hand. This could be anything from the position that chips are placed in, the lighting of a cigarette or the scratching of an ear.

Combating cheating

If you play in private games, be particularly wary of playing cards with strangers. Obviously you should not play in rooms with mirrors, but other reflective surfaces can allow a cheat to find out what cards players are holding. With the correct lighting, it is very easy to see what cards are being dealt to players if a table has a highly polished glass or marble surface. You should always, therefore, play on a table covered in felt or a cloth. Also check the light fittings, some glass lampshades act as excellent mirrors.

Always insist on checking the cards for marks before and after play. Watch the dealer carefully. Does he hold the cards in an unusual way. Someone dealing the second or bottom card is likely to cover the cards with his hands. Always cut the cards by inserting a card not in play, like a joker. This gets round the problem of someone bending one of the cards. Keep track of how much money goes into the pot. Carefully watch other players when they make their bets. Make sure they add the number of chips required. If you suspect other players of cheating, stop playing.

Burning of cards

Another way to try to combat cheating by the dealer is for several cards to be 'burnt'. The top five cards of a deck are removed and not used in play. However, a skilled technician can still shuffle the cards in such a way that his desired hand will be achieved.

To ensure fair play it is best to play card games in legal casinos. Here, new cards are used each day, and they are checked for marks before and after use. If cards do become marked during the course of play, they will be exchanged for new cards. The dealer controls all the betting and will ensure that the players contribute the correct number of chips. Cameras are installed on all the tables to record the action, so if you suspect either a player or the dealer of cheating, there is a record of the game which can be studied.

Shuffling and dealing the cards

To ensure the cards are really well mixed, it is best to use a combination of methods for shuffling. Laying the cards face down on the table and giving them a good mix is a good method of shuffling. This should be combined with a riffle shuffle. Here, the pack is split into two and your thumbs are used to riffle the cards so that the two halves are combined (see Figure 6.3).

The over hand style of shuffling where a number of cards are picked up from the back of the pack and dropped a few cards at a time to the front of the pack is most open to abuse as a technician can arrange the cards into virtually any desired order.

Invite a player to cut the cards. Ensure that none of the cards is exposed when you deal. Take particular care that the bottom card cannot be seen by any of the players. Angle the cards down towards the table when you deal. Take care not to reveal cards that have been discarded.

It is very important that players do not see either the card on the bottom of the pack or any discarded cards. If a player does see other cards he can use that information to his advantage. Suppose you see that the card on the bottom of the pack is a king. If you are dealt a pair of queens, you already know that the odds of being beaten by a pair of kings is reduced.

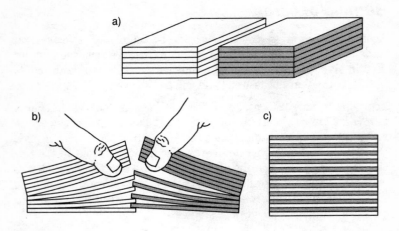

Figure 6.3 The riffle shuffle

7

THE DIFFERENT GAMES OF POKER

Five card draw

Each player receives five cards face down and after an initial round of betting has an opportunity to exchange any card in his hand for new cards from the deck. It is usual to select the cards that are being discarded and to return them to the dealer before new cards are drawn.

What hands should you play?

There is little point in staying in with anything lower than a high pair. A high pair may be enough to win without any improvement. If, for example, you stay in with a pair of sixes and take three cards in an attempt to get three of a kind, the odds against you achieving your desired hand are 7.5/1. Your opponent may have a pair of jacks and also has the same chance as you of improving. However, if neither of you improves he has already beaten your hand. If you still decide to stay in the game, you need to convince him that you got the desired cards on the draw. Your early bets may have given him no cause for concern. In order to be convincing you will need to make a big raise to force him out. If your bluff fails it may be costly.

You should be able to gain a fair indication of the types of hands held from the number of cards that each player exchanges. Also, if you compare the odds of being dealt a good hand in the first deal to the odds of improving on cards already held (see table below), you can see that the odds of improving are much better than the odds of having a good initial hand. So, if in the first deal you have nothing, it is better to withdraw from the game instead of exchanging all five cards. Even exchanging four cards needs something short of a miracle to give you a good hand. You will be betting against players who may already hold good cards and who, by exchanging one or two, can also improve.

Odds against improving hands in draw poker

Hand held	Cards drawn	Desired hand	Odds against achieving hand
Three of a kind	2	any improvement	17/2
Three of a kind + kicker	1	any improvement	11/1
Three of a kind	1	full house	15/1
Three of a kind	1	four of a kind	46/1
Three of a kind	2	full house	15/1
Three of a kind	2	four of a kind	23/1
Two pair	1	full house	11/1
One pair	3	three of a kind	7.5/1
One pair	3	full house	97/1
One pair	3	four of a kind	359/1
One pair + kicker	2	any improvement	3/1
One pair + kicker	2	two pair using kicker	7.5/1
One pair + kicker	2	two pair without kicker	17/1
One pair + kicker	2	three of a kind	12/1
One pair + kicker	2	full house	119/1
One pair + kicker	2	fours	1080/1
Four card flush	1	pair	3/1
Four card flush	1	flush	4.5/1
Four card incomplete straight flush (open ended)	1	straight or flush	2/1
		straight flush	22.5/1
Incomplete straight	1	any improvement	1/1
Flush (inside)		pair	3/1
		flush	5/1
		straight	11/1
		straight flush	46/1

Holding a pair

If you are holding a pair, you can improve your hand by exchanging up to three cards. However, if you exchange three cards, the other players will be immediately aware that you are likely to have a pair. Anyone with two pair or three of a kind will be confident that he has a better hand.

Instead of drawing three cards, you have the option of keeping a kicker. The 'kicker' will usually be your highest other card. Instead of exchanging three cards, you exchange two. Your chances of improving your hand are slightly reduced, but now the other players will be unsure as to whether you only have a pair or a possible three of a kind.

However, do not fall into the pattern of always retaining a kicker when you have a pair as the other players will soon work out your strategy. Vary your play as much as possible so that your opponents are never sure about your hand.

You may decide that the time is right to pull off a bluff. You may decide to take just one card to give an indication of a possible two pair that you are trying to improve to a full house or a possible flush. A big raise after drawing cards would be needed to back up the bluff.

Alternatively, you may decide to take no cards. The players will be aware that you may have been dealt a very good hand, but again, they cannot be certain. They will be aware of the odds against you obtaining a high ranking hand with just five cards, but if you are known as a player who rarely bluffs then you may be successful. However, if you have bluffed too often in the past, you are unlikely to get away with another bluff.

Holding three of a kind

You have the choice of exchanging either one or both cards. You have a greater chance of improving to a full house or four of a kind by taking two cards. However, if you always take two cards you will alert the other players to the fact that you are likely to have three of a kind. If, instead, you occasionally exchange one card, keeping a kicker, you will keep the other players guessing.

Holding a full house

It is pointless trying to improve to four of a kind. You already hold a hand which is going to be very difficult for other players to beat, and so your real decision should be whether to raise before the draw to force out other players who may improve on the draw.

Example game

Figure 7.1 shows the hands of four players before and after the draw.

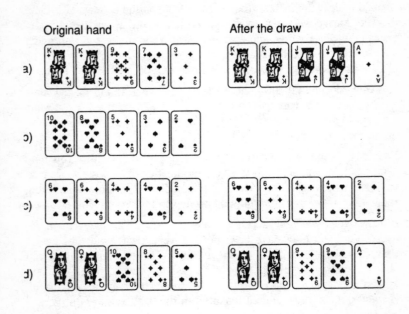

Figure 7.1 Example of draw poker hands

Player A has been dealt a good initial hand with a pair of kings. Three cards are drawn. He fails to get three of a kind but gets another pair. The fifth card is an ace. He knows that even if another player has a pair of aces, the fact that he is holding an ace makes it harder for him to achieve three of a kind.

Player B has a poor initial hand so decides to fold.

Player C has two pair. Although the cards are low, he has the opportunity of making a full house by drawing one card. He has seen player

A draw three cards, so he knows that A's initial hand is a pair. He fails to improve his hand.

Player D has a high pair of two queens. He is aware that A also initially had a pair. Player C only took one card so he is possibly going for a full house, a flush, a straight, or is bluffing. D draws three cards and improves to two pair.

Player A raises. Player C decides to fold. He realises that play A may have improved, possibly to three of a kind or two pair. Although player C has two pair, they are low value cards.

Player D knows he has a fairly good hand so he raises player A. He knows two pair with kings or aces could beat him but he holds an ace so knows the chances of player A holding a pair of aces or three aces is reduced.

The game now becomes a test of nerves between A and D. If either backs down then the other will win the pot. If the game continues to a showdown then player A will win the showdown.

Five card stud

Each player receives five cards from which they make their best five card poker hand. Initially each player is dealt one card face up and one face down. The player with the lowest face-up card must make a forced bet. The remaining cards are dealt face up. A round of betting takes place after each card has been dealt. The player showing the highest ranking hand is the first to bet in each round.

Here you progressively get more information on which to base your decisions. Once all the cards have been dealt you should have a pretty good idea of your opponents' likely hands.

Strategy

If you cannot match or better the highest card showing you should fold. Ideally aim for a minimum hand of a high pair.

See Figure 7.2. In the initial deal, player B has the lowest face-up card so makes a forced bet. As each card is dealt more information is known about each player's hand. By the fourth card players A, C and

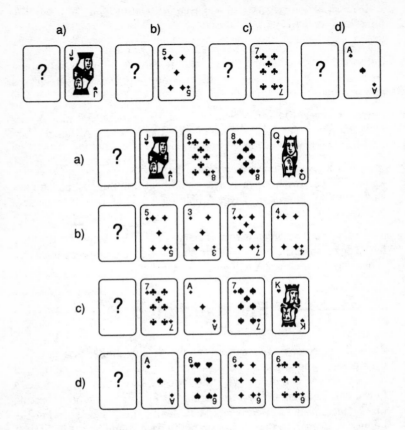

Figure 7.2 Examples of five card stud hands

D are all showing pairs. Player B has the potential to achieve a straight flush.

By the time the fifth card has been dealt, it is clear what the possible hands might be. The best hands are A – three of a kind with eights, B – a straight flush, C – three of a kind with sevens, and D – four of a kind with sixes. If each player achieves his best possible hand then player B would win on a showdown.

Each player needs to assess their chances of winning against the other hands.

If player A has another 8, he is certain of beating player C. He also knows that if B has any card other than a diamond then his hand is nothing. If player D's hole card (the card dealt face down) is not a 6 or an ace then player A will also beat him. One of the aces is revealed in player C's hand, which gives D less chance of achieving a full house.

Player B knows that he has potentially the best hand. If his hole card is not a diamond then whether or not he wins will depend on how well he can bluff.

If player C has another 7, he will have to decide whether or not the other players are bluffing. Although all the players have the potential for good hands it is unlikely that they have all achieved them. If the other players are all bluffing, player C would win a showdown.

Seven card stud

Seven card stud is the one of the most popular forms of poker. Each player receives seven cards. The aim is to make the best possible five card poker hand from the seven cards dealt to you. The player with the best hand wins all the money staked, less the rake (a charge made by the casino for the use of its facilities).

Initially three cards are dealt, two face down and one face up. The fourth, fifth and sixth cards are dealt face up, and the seventh face down. You therefore have four cards on display to the other players and three cards which are hidden from view.

There is a round of betting after each card has been dealt. The person with the highest ranking poker hand on view is the first to either bet or fold in each round of betting. So, someone with three of a kind would be the first to bet if all the other players are showing one pair.

Here, you have quite a lot of useful information on which to base your strategy. You may be able to deduce from the other players' four cards on display that your hand has no chance of winning. You can use your knowledge of the odds to calculate your opponents' chance of completing hands that are shown. However, the other players can also deduce the same amount of information from your cards on view.

If your cards on display show the potential for a good hand which could beat the likely hands of all the other players, but you do not hold the cards necessary, you have the option to bluff. By continually raising the stakes you may force the other players to fold. The game then becomes a test of nerves. The other players will realise what your potential hand is and will see that you are betting heavily. They will then have to decide whether or not you are bluffing. If you force all the other players to fold, your hand will not be revealed and they will never know that you were bluffing. If, however, a showdown is reached, your cards will be revealed.

Example hands

Figure 7.3 Examples of seven card stud hands

See Figure 7.3. Suppose you are player A. You have two pair. You can immediately see that player B has a better hand with three of a kind. Player C also has a pair which beats your hand, but could have a full house if he has either another king or another five. In the cards that you are showing, you have the 9, 8 and 7 of hearts. Although your hand can't win in a showdown against either A or B, by using a heavy round of betting you could convince them that you have the other two cards necessary to complete a straight flush.

Hold 'em

Each player receives two cards face down. Five cards are then placed face up in the centre of the table, and these cards are used by all the players. Each player uses any combination of the two cards in his hand and the five community cards to make the best five card poker hand.

The deal

Initially each player receives his two hidden cards followed by a round of betting. Players often have the opportunity to bet blind (to place a bet before they look at their cards). This helps to increase the pot. Three of the community cards are then dealt, called the 'flop'. Another round of betting follows. A further community card is dealt followed by a round of betting, then the final community card is dealt.

Since each player's cards are hidden from view, the only indication you have of their possible hands is the way in which they are betting. In order to make a proper assessment, you really need to see all of the community cards first. Once you have seen these, you are then in a better position to assess the likely hands.

Strategy before the flop

You need to decide whether or not your two cards are worth playing. In general terms it is worth while playing any pair, consecutive cards of the same suit, such as 9, 8 or 6, 5 and fairly high cards of the same suit, such as J, 9.

Strategy after the flop

You now have a better indication of the possible hands. You can assess your position against all the other possibilities. If the community cards have not helped you, they may well have given other players the possibility of really good hands. If this is the situation then fold now.

If you are still in a fairly good position, you need to force out anyone who can beat you either now or once the other two cards have been dealt.

Nuts

Occasionally a situation may arise where you know that you have the best possible hand (nuts) that can be made using the community cards. There is no way that you can be beaten. Clearly in this situation you want to maximise the pot. Your strategy for betting will need to be based on your knowledge of the players. You need to keep the betting at the right level to keep as many of the players betting as possible (see Figure 7.4)

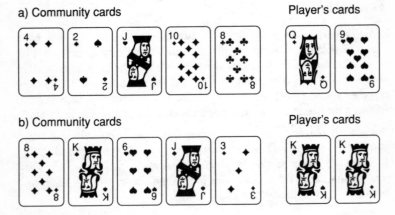

Figure 7.4 'Nuts'

Example hands

See figure 7.5. The best possible hand from the community cards is four of a kind, followed by a full house then three of a kind.

Player A will deduce that he has a good hand with three of a kind. He knows that he has the best possible three of a kind and can only be beaten by a full house and since he holds one of the aces, the chances of anyone holding either two queens, two fours or two threes are low.

However, player B has a full house. He knows that only four of a kind or a full house with queens or fours could beat him.

Player C has nothing and would be wise to fold. Betting would then commence between A and B. It would probably develop into a test of nerves to determine who would fold, or alternatively would ultimately lead to a showdown which B would win.

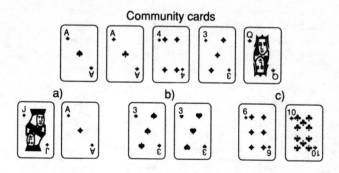

Figure 7.5 Example of hold 'em hands

Omaha

Each player receives four cards face down. Five cards are then placed face up in the centre of the table to be used by all the players. Each player uses any combination of two cards in his hand and three community cards to make the best five card poker hand.

The game is dealt in a similar way to hold 'em with a flop of three cards. You may also be given the opportunity to bet blind (to bet before looking at your cards). What makes the game more complicated is the way in which the five card poker hand is made. When you see the cards you need to give some thought as to what hand you have actually got. At first glance you may seem to have an exceptionally good hand. But you need to remember that you can only use two of the cards in your hand (see Figure 7.6).

By looking at the cards in total, player A can immediately see a full house (three fours and two tens). However, because only two cards can be used from his hand he only has two pair (two tens and two fours).

Player B appears to have a straight (A, K, Q, J, 10) but the hand actually held is two pair (two jacks and two tens).

At first glance player C may appear to have a full house (three twos and two tens). However, he can only use two cards from his hand so only holds two pairs (two tens and two twos).

Community cards

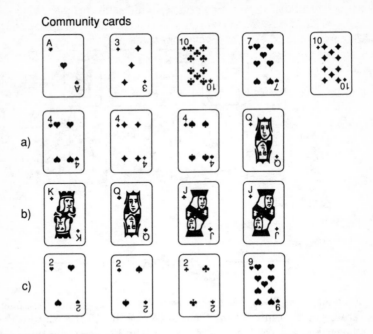

Figure 7.6 Example of omaha hands

From the community cards, you can obtain a lot of information about the possible hands held by other players. In Figure 7.6, the possible hands are: four of a kind – one player has the other two tens; a full house – one player has one 10 and an ace, 7 or 3 or holds two of the other aces, sevens or threes; three of a kind – one of the other tens, or a pair of aces, sevens or threes; two pair – a player holds another pair or one ace, 7 or 2.

Strategy

The strategy is similar to hold 'em. You really need to see the flop before you can make any decision. However, a situation can arise when it is wise to fold immediately after you have been dealt your hole cards.

Being dealt four of a kind in your hole cards is one of the worst possible situations. You can only use two cards so at best you have a pair with no chance of improving on them. Being dealt three of a kind also gives you only a remote chance that the fourth card will appear in the community cards. The same is true of being dealt four cards to a possible flush; your chances of making the flush are drastically reduced.

Figure 7.7 Hands to fold on in omaha

The best cards to play with are high pairs or high cards of the same suit (if you hold only two of the same suit) which could lead to a flush.

After the flop, you will be in a much better position to judge your chances of winning. Then you can assess all of the possibilities and work out your chances of making a good hand. It is at this stage that you need to force out anyone who has the potential to improve his hand into one that could beat yours.

Nuts

As with hold 'em, occasionally a situation may arise where you know that you have the best possible hand (nuts) that can be made using the community cards. There is no way that you can be beaten. Clearly in this situation you want to maximise the pot. Your strategy for betting will need to be based on your knowledge of the players. You need to keep betting at the right level to keep as many of the players betting as possible.

—— Caribbean stud poker ——

The games we have looked at so far all involve betting against the other players – you have to beat everyone else playing in order to win the pot. Caribbean stud poker differs because it is a banking game. Instead of playing against other players you are playing against the casino which acts as a bank, paying out all winning bets. The casino provides a dealer. In order to win, you have only to beat the dealer's hand. The other players' hands do not affect the outcome of your bets.

The game

The object of the game is to win by having a five card poker hand that ranks higher than the dealer's. Each player makes an ante-bet and is dealt five cards face down. The dealer receives four cards face down and one card face up.

Players then look at their cards and have the option to play or fold. If a player folds, his ante-bet is lost. If a player decides to continue, he must then make a further bet of double his ante-bet.

The dealer will then reveal his hand. He must have an ace and a king or higher in order to play his hand. If a player's hand beats the dealer's, the ante-bet is paid at evens. See the table below for the odds for the second bet. If the dealer does not have at least an ace and a king then a player is paid even money on the ante-bet and the additional bet is void (not lost). If, however, the dealer's hand beats the player's, then both bets are lost.

Payout odds for an additional bet in Caribbean stud poker	
One pair or less	1/1 (even)
Two pair	2/1
Three of a kind	3/1
Straight	4/1
Flush	5/1
Full house	7/1
Four of a kind	20/1
Straight flush	50/1
Royal flush	100/1

_____ him in the dining room with
_____ potatoes and peas or something. Besides
_____ of pimples. Not just on his forehead or his chin,
_____ ays, but all over his whole face. And not only that, he
_____ rrible personality. He was also sort of a nasty guy. I
_____ too crazy about him, to tell you the truth.

_____ could feel him standing on the shower ledge, right behind my
_hair, taking a look to see if Stradlater was around. He hated
Stradlater's guts and he never came in the room if Stradlater was
around. He hated _ev_erybody's guts, damn near.

He came down off the shower ledge and came in the room. 'Hi,'
he said. He always said it like he was terrifically bored or
terrifically tired. He didn't want you to think he was _vis_iting you
or anything. He wanted you to think he'd come in by mis_take_, for
God's sake.

'Hi,' I said, but I didn't look up from my book. With a guy like
Ackley, if you looked up from your book you were a goner. You
were a goner _any_way, but not as quick if you didn't look up right
away.

He started walking around the room, very slow and all, the
way he always did, picking up your personal stuff off your desk
and chiffonier. He always picked up your personal stuff and
looked at it. Boy, could he get on your nerves sometimes. 'How
was the fencing?' he said. He just wanted me to quit reading and
enjoying myself. He didn't give a damn about the fencing. 'We
win, or what?' he said.

'Nobody won,' I said. Without looking up, though.

'What?' he said. He always made you say everything twice.

'Nobody won,' I said. I sneaked a look to see what he was fiddling
around with on my chiffonier. He was looking at this picture of this
girl I used to go around with in New York, Sally Hayes. He must've
picked up that goddam picture and looked at it at least five thousand
times since I got it. He always put it back in the wrong place, too,
___en he was finished. He did it on purpose. You could tell.

_____ won,' he said. 'How come?'

_____ dam foils and stuff on the subway.' I still didn't

We got on the

at a goddam map on

He came over and stoo

read this same sentence about th

Anybody else except Ackley wou_____ken the goddam hint.
Not him, though. 'Think they'll make you pay for 'em?' he said.

'I don't know, and I don't give a damn. How 'bout sitting
down or something, Ackley kid? You're right in my goddam
light.' He didn't like it when you called him 'Ackley kid.' He was
always telling me I was a goddam kid, because I was sixteen and
he was eighteen. It drove him mad when I called him 'Ackley kid.'

He kept standing there. He was ex*act*ly the kind of a guy that
wouldn't get out of your light when you asked him to. He'd *do* it,
finally, but it took him a lot longer if you *asked* him to. 'What the
hellya reading?' he said.

'Goddam book.'

He shoved my book back with his hand so that he could see the
name of it. 'Any good?' he said.

'This *sent*ence I'm reading is terrific.' I can be quite sarcastic
when I'm in the mood. He didn't get it, though. He started
walking around the room again, picking up all my personal stuff,
and Stradlater's. Finally, I put my book down on the floor.
You couldn't read anything with a guy like Ackley around. It was impossible.

I slid way the hell down in my chair and watched old Ackley
making himself at home. I was feeling sort of tired from the trip
to New York and all, and I started yawning. Then I started
horsing around a little bit. Sometimes I horse around quite a lot,
just to keep from getting bored. What I did was, I pulled the old
peak of my hunting hat around to the front, then pulled it way
down over my eyes. That way, I couldn't see a goddam thing. 'I
think I'm going blind,' I said in this very hoarse voice. 'Mother
darling, everything's getting so *dark* in here.'

'You're nuts. I swear to God,' Ackley said.

'Mother darling, give me your *hand*. Why won't you give me
your *hand*?'

If the dealer and the player play the same poker hand, the remaining cards are taken into consideration. If all five cards are equal, the hand is void (the bet is not lost). Neither the ante-bet or the additional bet are paid. The type of suit makes no difference to the hand.

The disadvantage of this game is that you are relying purely on luck. There is no skill involved. You do not have the opportunity to bluff. In poker games where you are playing for a pot, you are still able to win even with a poor hand but with Caribbean stud poker, if you have a poor hand, you stand little chance of winning.

The minimum odds in this game are evens. In a normal game of poker with, for example, seven players you would have odds of at least 6/1 and quite often a great deal better.

The odds paid for the additional bet are also poor compared to the chances of achieving them. Odds of 100/1 are paid for a royal flush, yet your chances of being dealt one are 649,739/1. The only advantage you have is that you know how much each game is going to cost you.

Caribbean stud poker should only be played for amusement purposes. If you want to win money, you are better off playing games where you are contesting for a pot.

Pai gow poker

In pai gow poker each player in turn has the option of being banker. The game is a mixture of the Chinese game pai gow and American poker. It is played with one deck of 52 cards, plus one joker. The joker can be used only as an ace, or to complete a straight, a flush, a straight flush, or a royal flush.

The casino provides the dealer. Each player is dealt seven cards. The cards are arranged to make two hands; a two card hand and a five card hand. The five card hand must rank higher or be equal to the two card hand (see table of rankings overleaf).

The object of the game is for both of your hands to rank higher than both of your opponent's hands. Your two card hand must rank higher than your opponent's two card hand and your five card hand must rank higher than your opponent's five card hand.

Ranking of hands in pai gow poker

Five card hand	*Two card hand*
Five aces (five aces plus the joker)	One pair
Royal flush	High card
Straight flush	
Four of a kind	
Full house	
Flush	
Straight	
Three of a kind	
Two pair	
One pair	
High card	

If one of your hands ranks the same as your opponent's hand, this is a tie (or copy hand). The banker wins all ties. If you win one hand but lose the other, this is known as a 'push'. In push hands no money is exchanged. Winning hands are paid even money less a five per cent commission. Losing hands lose the money bet.

The game

The dealer and each player in turn are all given the opportunity to be banker. You can only be banker if you bet against the dealer the last time he was banker. You need to have sufficient chips to pay the bets should your opponent win.

You arrange your cards into the two hands and place them face down on the table. Once you've put them down, you can no longer touch them. The dealer will turn over his cards and make his hands. Each hand is compared to the dealer's hands. If the player wins one hand and loses the other, the bet is void (a push). If you wrongly set your hand – you lose.

The major disadvantage to this game is that you are relying on the luck of the deal – there is no skill involved. If your cards are poor, there is no opportunity to bluff. The dealer plays his hand if he has the minimum required and does not drop out of the betting.

As with Caribbean stud poker, the odds are also poor compared to playing with a pot.

Dealer's hands

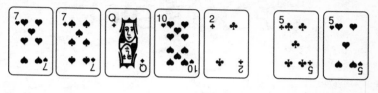

Player's hands

Figure 7.8 Examples of pai gow poker hands

See Figure 7.8. Player A has beaten the dealer's five card hand but has failed to beat the two card hand. This is a push – the money bet is not lost.

Player B has beaten both hands. His bet is paid at even money less five per cent commission.

Player C has failed to beat the dealer's five and two card hand. He loses his bet.

8

POKER DICE

Dice can also be used to play poker. Five dice are used. The faces of the dice are marked with ace, king, queen, jack, 10 and 9. Although the game can be played with two players, it is more practical when played with between three and six players.

Figure 8.1 The symbols on the faces of the dice

The throws are ranked in the following descending order:

Five of a kind
Four of a kind
Full house
High straight / Big street
Low straight / Small street
Three of a kind
Two pair
One pair

The game is played with a cup/hat which covers the dice, and which sits on a felt-covered saucer. The equipment allows each player in turn to look at the dice without revealing them to the other players.

Figure 8.2 The equipment for playing dice poker

Betting

There are several options for betting. Often the game is played in pubs for rounds of drinks. The loser is the one who buys a round for all the other players. Alternatively, the loser pays an agreed amount to each player.

Playing the game

Each player throws a dice, the one with the highest score goes first. The player puts all of the dice under the hat and shakes them. He announces his hand and passes the dice to the player sitting on either his left or right.

The game then continues in the direction selected (clockwise or anti-clockwise). The next player has the option of either accepting the throw or refusing it. If he refuses it, he removes the hat revealing the dice to all the other players. If the throw is equal to or more than that announced, the second player loses.

If the player accepts the throw, he must pass on a higher ranking throw to the next player. To get a higher ranking hand he is allowed to shake either all or some of the dice.

Dice may be removed from the hat and the remaining dice shaken, or dice may be left under the hat and some removed and thrown on the table. Players must always pass on a higher ranking hand. Even if you do not have a higher ranking hand, you can bluff.

Example game

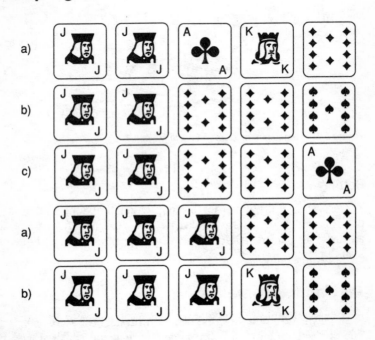

Figure 8.3 Example of poker dice game

Figure 8.3 shows the throws made by three players – A, B and C.

Player A goes first, he shakes all the dice, looks at what he has thrown and announces two jacks.

Player B accepts the throw and looks at the dice. He removes the jacks from the hat and places them on the table. He then shakes the remaining dice and looks at them. He announces two jacks, two tens and a nine.

Player C removes the two tens from the hat and places them on the table. The remaining dice is shaken in an attempt to get a full house. Although he fails to get a full house he has managed to beat B's throw. He announces two jacks, two tens and an ace.

Player A accepts this and also attempts to get a full house by shaking the remaining dice. He throws a jack and gets a full house. He announces three jacks and two tens or a full house jacks over tens.

Player B accepts. He removes the third jack from the hat and places it on the table. He puts the two tens under the hat and shakes the dice. To beat the full house he needs to throw two queens, two kings, two aces or another jack. He actually throws a king and a nine. This is not enough to beat the previous score so he lies and announces three jacks and two queens.

Player C refuses to accept and removes the hat. The bluff is revealed and player B loses.

Keeping score

Cards are usually used to keep the score. As the game is often played in pubs, beer mats are used. A player who loses a game receives a card. When all the cards have been used, players then return them when they win. The object of the game is to end up with no cards. The first player to get rid of all his cards is the winner. Players with no cards drop out of the game. The last player remaining is the loser.

Number of cards used

Players will usually agree between themselves how many cards will be used. As a rough guide, for two to three players six cards should be used and for four to six players, eight cards should be used.

With each new game the direction of play can be changed, as the first player decides whether to go clockwise or anti-clockwise. Once all the cards have been distributed, the direction of play can no longer be changed.

GLOSSARY

Ante – a bet made before any cards have been dealt
Babies – small value cards
Bicycle – see wheel
Blind bet – a bet made without looking at your cards
Bluff – tricking the other players into thinking that you have a really good hand
Board – the community cards in games such as hold 'em and omaha
Bone – another name for a chip
Bug – a joker
Bullet – an ace
Burnt card – a card which is removed from the pack and not used in play. Often several of the top cards will be removed before hands are dealt to combat cheating by the dealer
Button – a plastic marker used in casino games to denote an imaginery dealer to ensure that no player gains an advantage from his position relative to the actual dealer
By me – a verbal statement in draw poker that a player is not exchanging any cards
Call – a verbal statement that a player will match the previous bet
Calling station – a player who hardly ever raises
Chip – a plastic disc used in place money for betting
Community cards – cards which can be used by all the players to make up their best five card poker hand in games such as hold 'em and omaha
Commission – a charge made by the casino for the use of its facilities, usually a percentage of the pot
Dead man's hand – two pair of aces over eights

Deuce – two

Door card – in stud poker the first card that is dealt face up

Draw – exchanging cards in your hand for cards from the deck

Fives – five cards of the same value – this hand is only possible where wild cards are used

Flop – the deal where the first three community cards are revealed in hold 'em and omaha

Flush – five cards of the same suit

Fold – withdraw from the game

Fours – four cards of the same value, for example, four queens

Freak – a wild card

Full house – three cards of the same value with a pair, for example, three aces and two sixes

Hole cards – a player's cards which are dealt face down

House advantage – an adjustment made to the odds on banking games which allows the casino to make a profit

Kicker – in draw poker this is a card retained to make it more difficult for your opponents to guess your hand

Knave – a jack

Knock – in draw poker a player may knock on the table to signify that no cards are required

Limit – the maximum bet

Low poker – a game where players aim to have the lowest ranking poker hand

Marked cards – cards which have been marked in some way so that a cheat can identify their values from looking at their backs

Monster – a high ranking hand

Muck pile – the pile of cards from players who have folded

Nuts – having a hand in games such as hold 'em and omaha which is the best possible hand and which cannot be beaten by any other player

Odds – a ratio expressing your chances of losing against your chances of winning, for example, odds of 2/1 means you have two chances of losing against 1 chance of winning

Open – to place the first bet

Openers – cards needed to open a pot, for example, two jacks are needed to open a jackpot. In some games, a minimum hand is needed before an opening bet can be made. In a jackpot, two jacks are needed, for a queen pot – two queens, etc.

Over – used as a short way of expressing two pair, for example, queens *over* tens means two queens and two tens

Paint – any court card, for example, king, queen or jack

Pig – a high and low hand

Pocket cards – cards which are dealt face down

Poker face – having complete control over your facial expressions so that you do not give your opponents any clues about your hand

Rake – a charge made by the casino for the use of its facilities, usually a percentage of the pot

River – the last round of betting

Rock – a player who always folds unless he has a really good hand

Run – another name for a straight

Runt – a hand lower than a pair

School – a group of players who regularly play poker together

See – has the same meaning as 'call'

Set – three cards of the same value

Showdown – when the players reveal their hands

Sitting pat – a player who takes no cards in draw poker

Stake – the amount of money bet

Straddle – a method of betting where the previous bet is doubled – the doubling of previous bets usually continues for a pre-determined number of times

Straight – five cards of any suit in consecutive order

Street – a round of betting – first street is the first round of betting, second street the second and so on

Stud – a form of poker where some cards are dealt face up

Sweeten – to add money to the pot, usually in the form of an ante-bet

Technician – someone who is skilled at manipulating the cards so that he can deal himself a good hand

Threes – three cards of the same value

Trips – three cards of the same value

Trey – a three

Wheel – 5, 4, 3, 2, A in low poker

Wild cards – a nominated card which can be used in place of any other card to form a poker hand

APPENDIX

Gamblers Anonymous organisations —— in Great Britain, Australia —— and the United States

Great Britain
Gamblers Anonymous
National Service Office
PO Box 88
London
SW10 0EU
Tel: 0171 384 3040

United States
Gamblers Intergroup
PO Box 7
New York
New York 10116
Tel: (212) 265 8600

Australia
Gamblers Anonymous
Head Office
Corner of Dorcas and Montague Street
South Melbourne
Tel: (3) 696 6108

Gamblers Anonymous
PO Box Burwood
Sydney
NSW 2134
Tel: (02) 564 1574

INDEX

How to Win at **CARD GAMES**

Belinda Levez

This short course will give you a basic knowledge of gambling card games. Belinda Levez is a former casino croupier. In this book she shares her inside knowledge to help you maximise your winnings. All the main games are covered

- blackjack
- baccarat chemin de fer
- poker
- punto banco
- five card draw
- five card stud
- seven card stud
- hold'em
- omaha
- caribbean stud poker
- pai gow poker
- red dog

This book will be a real help both for those who know nothing about gambling and betting and for those with some experience who want to learn more and improve the odds for success.

How to Win at
CASINO GAMES

Belinda Levez

This short course will give you a basic knowledge of casino gambling. Belinda Levez is a former casino croupier. In this book she shares her inside knowledge to help you maximise your winnings. All the main games are covered

- roulette
- blackjack
- punto banco
- dice/craps
- poker
- two up

This book will be a real help both for those who know nothing about gambling and for those with some experience who want to learn more and improve the odds for success.

Other related titles

 TEACH YOURSELF

How to Win at
HORSE RACING

Belinda Levez

This short course will give you a basic knowledge of betting on horse racing. Belinda Levez is a former betting shop manager. In this book she shares her inside knowledge to help you maximise your winnings. All the main areas of betting are covered

- off-course betting
- tote betting
- bookmaking
- selecting winners
- getting the best price
- betting strategies
- calculating winnings
- ready reckoner

This book will be a real help both for those who know nothing about betting and for those with some experience who want to learn more and improve the odds for success.

HP

Richmond upon Thames Libraries

Renew online at www.richmond.gov.uk/libraries

LONDON BOROUGH OF
RICHMOND UPON THAMES

90710 000 537 744